The Cat Fight

By Clem King

It was Friday night,
and Dad had made a treat!

“Hi, Sky,” he said.
“I made a plum pie!”

"What a sight," Sky sighed.
"What a smell!"

Then there was a big cry!

Sky's two cats rolled in.
They were **mad**.

Faith hit Bligh!

Bligh hissed at Faith!

Hiss!
F
B

The cats were in a fight!

Faith and Bligh ran up onto the bench.

They were so close to Dad's pie!

You cats gave me a big fright!
F

Faith hit the stand,
and the pie fell from up high!

Some pie landed right
by Sky.

"The pie!" called Sky.

"Sky, my pie!" said Dad.

"It was not me!" said Sky.
"I would not lie, Dad."

Dad could see the cats.

“I must get the pie away from those cats!” he said. “They might eat it all!”

"Help me fix this mess,"
said Dad.

"We can try to save
some pie," said Sky.

Dad set out the sweet pie for him, Sky and Mum.

"What is **this**?" said Mum.

"It is smashed pie!" said Sky.

CHECKING FOR MEANING

1. When did Dad make the pie? *(Literal)*
2. How did the pie fall on the floor? *(Literal)*
3. How do you think Sky was feeling when Dad came in and saw the fallen pie? *(Inferential)*

EXTENDING VOCABULARY

night	Look at the word *night*. How many letters are in the word? How many sounds? What word means the opposite of *night*?
sighed	What does the word *sighed* mean? Why does Sky sigh in the story? When have you sighed? How were you feeling?
lie	What is the meaning of the word *lie* in the story? What other meaning can *lie* have?

MOVING BEYOND THE TEXT

1. The weekend begins on Friday night. What activities do you do when the school week is over?
2. What might Dad do differently next time he makes a pie?
3. Do you have a favourite food? What is your favourite treat to eat?
4. What words do you know that describe the sounds that cats make? What are some sounds that other animals make?

TIME TO WRITE

Write about why the cat fight might have started.

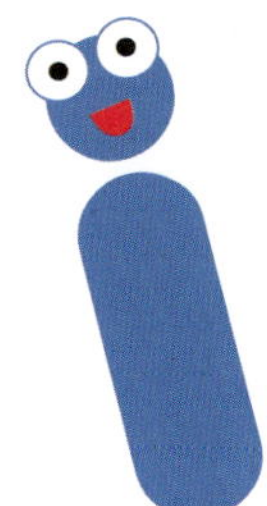

PRACTICE WORDS

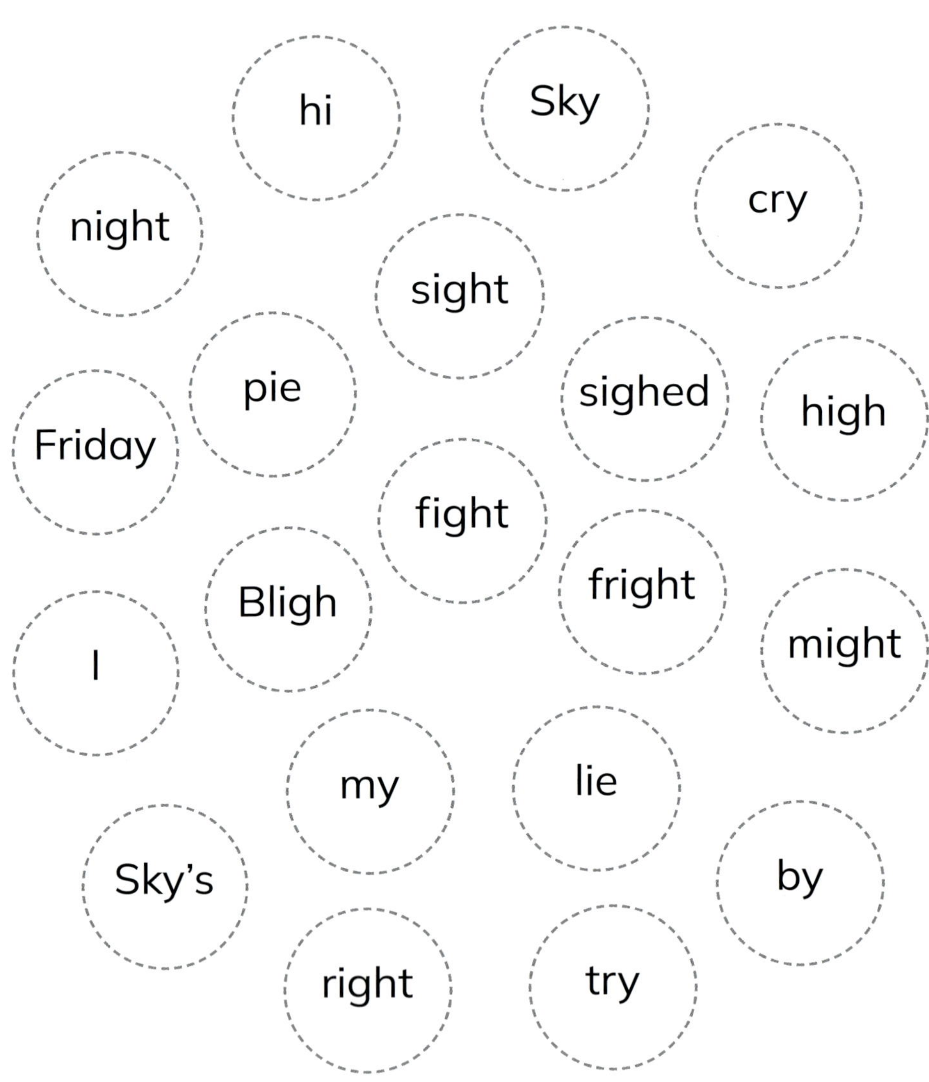